LEWIS & CLARK

THE MOUNTAINS

JOHN HAMILTON

VISIT US AT

WWW.ABDOPUB.COM

Published by ABDO & Daughters, an imprint of ABDO Publishing Company, 4940 Viking Drive, Suite 622, Edina, Minnesota 55435. Copyright ©2003 by Abdo Consulting Group, Inc. International copyrights reserved in all countries. No part of this book may be reproduced in any form without written permission from the publisher.

Printed in the United States.

Edited by Paul Joseph
Graphic Design: John Hamilton
Cover Design: Mighty Media
Photos and illustrations:
    John Hamilton, Cover, p. 1, 4-13, 16, 18-20, 23, 25-30
    Beinecke Museum, Andrew Russell, p. 15
    John F. Clymer, Clymer Museum of Art, p. 6, 22-23
    Library of Congress, W. Clark, p. 3, 30-31
    Library of Congress, E.S. Curtis, p. 29
    Montana Historical Society, Charles M. Russell, p. 24
    Charles Willson Peale, p. 21
    C. M. Russell Museum, p. 17
    N. C. Wyeth, p. 14

Library of Congress Cataloging-in-Publication Data

Hamilton, John, 1959-
    The mountains / John Hamilton.
    p. cm.—(Lewis & Clark)
    Includes bibliographical references and index.
    Summary: Joins the Lewis and Clark Expedition in the summer of 1805 as it leaves the Three Forks of the Missouri area and travels through the Bitterroot Mountains. Includes highlights and directions to historical points of interest.
    ISBN 1-57765-764-0
    1. Lewis and Clark Expedition (1804-1806)—Juvenile literature. 2. West (U.S.)—Discovery and exploration—Juvenile literature. 3. West (U.S.)—Description and travel—Juvenile literature. 4. Rocky Mountains—Description and travel—Juvenile literature. [1. Lewis and Clark Expedition (1804-1806) 2. West (U.S.)—Discovery and exploration. 3. Rocky Mountains—Description and travel.] I. Title.

F592.7.H273 2002
917.804'2—dc21

    2001053396

TABLE OF CONTENTS

THE JEFFERSON

On August 12, 1805, President Thomas Jefferson received a shipment of materials from Lewis and Clark. They had sent the shipment the previous spring while at the Mandan Indian villages in present-day North Dakota. The shipment included Indian corn, elk antlers (which still hang at Jefferson's home at Monticello, Virginia), maps, journals, and two live animals that survived the trip: a magpie and a prairie dog.

After reading Meriwether Lewis's report, Jefferson felt confident. He guessed the Corps of Discovery was already safely camped on the coast of the Pacific Ocean. In reality, they weren't even close.

 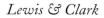

By the end of July 1805, the expedition had made it to the Three Forks, the point where three major tributaries of the Missouri River come together.

Lewis and Clark named the three tributaries the Gallatin, after Secretary of the Treasury Albert Gallatin; the Madison, after Secretary of State James Madison; and the Jefferson. In his journal, Lewis wrote that they called it the Jefferson River "in honor of that illustrious personage Thomas Jefferson, the author of our enterprise." The captains agreed that the right-hand fork, the Jefferson, was the river to follow, since it appeared to lead toward the Rocky Mountains.

Captain William Clark estimated they had traveled almost 2,500 miles (4,023 km) from St. Louis. Captain Lewis wrote in his journal that the Three Forks was "an essential point in the geography of this western part of the continent."

The Jefferson River, just above the Three Forks of the Missouri, in southwestern Montana

Lewis took careful readings to mark the Three Forks's exact latitude and longitude, and suggested in his notes that the area would make a good location for a fort. The Corps spent two days at the Three Forks, recuperating and repairing their canoes and equipment.

Sacagawea was the teenage wife of their interpreter and cook, Toussaint Charbonneau. She told the captains they were close to the spot where she had been kidnapped by a war party of Hidatsa Indians five years earlier. This lifted the spirits of Lewis and Clark. Sacagawea was a member of the Shoshone nation, which the captains knew kept large herds of ponies.

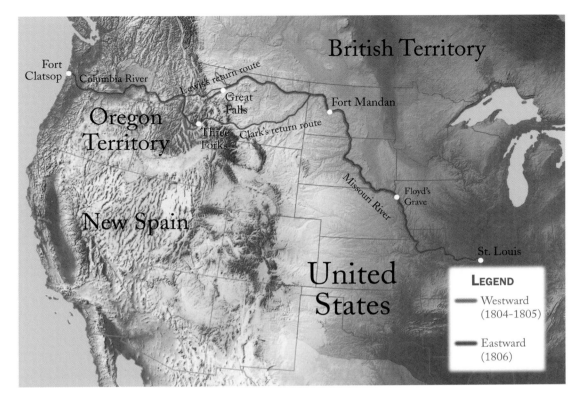

With any luck, they hoped to trade for some of the horses. These would carry the men and supplies over the Continental Divide to the Columbia River system, which led to the Pacific Ocean. But first, they had to locate the Shoshone Indians.

The Jefferson River led west, toward the mountains. It was a clear, swift-flowing stream. The men struggled to pull their dugout canoes up the shallow water. The going was miserable. Gnats and mosquitoes swarmed their faces. They slipped on the rocky riverbed and sprained their ankles and knees. Ropes they used to drag the canoes snapped. Joseph Whitehouse was nearly drowned when a canoe floated over him, trapping him between the streambed and the bottom of the boat.

Prickly pear cacti sliced through the men's moccasins. William Clark's feet had become infected, and a large boil on his ankle made him nearly unable to walk. Still, the Corps pressed on toward the mountains.

This is a replica of Meriwether Lewis's espontoon. In addition to using the steel-pointed staff for self-defense, Lewis also used it to steady his rifle, which helped him to shoot more accurately. In the background is a Native American tepee, similar to the one Lewis and Clark slept in after visiting the Mandan villages of present-day North Dakota. Sacagawea, along with her husband and baby, also slept in the tepee.

"August 2nd. The tops of these mountains [are] yet partially covered with snow, while we in the valley [are] suffocated nearly with the intense heat of the midday sun. The nights are so cold that two blankets are not more than sufficient covering… Capt. Clark discovered a tumor rising on the inner side of his ankle this evening, which was painfull to him"

MERIWETHER LEWIS

The Jefferson forked into smaller streams. Sometimes the Corps took the wrong path, then had to double back several miles. Many of the men wanted to stop dragging the canoes up the river and go instead by foot.

After a week of this torture, there was still no sign of the Shoshones or their horses. The only piece of good news came from Sacagawea, who recognized a rock outcropping called Beaverhead Rock, near present-day Dillon, Montana. They were definitely on the right track.

Beaverhead Rock, near Dillon, Montana

"*Further [up was] the most distant fountain of the waters of the Mighty Missouri, in surch of which we have spent so many toilsome days and wristless nights.*"

MERIWETHER LEWIS

THE MOST DISTANT FOUNTAIN

Meriwether Lewis was desperate to contact the Shoshones and secure horses for the mountain trek. On August 9, he and a small group of men set out on foot ahead of the main party. Two days later, they spotted a lone Native American on horseback, the first they had seen since leaving the Mandan villages that spring.

The man stopped some distance away; he seemed suspicious of the strangers. Lewis walked slowly forward, trying to signal that they were friendly. Suddenly, the man turned his horse and vanished into the woods. Perhaps he thought Lewis and his men were Blackfeet or Hidatsa warriors. Whatever the reason, Lewis's hopes were dashed. But still they pressed on.

The next day, August 12, 1805, the same day President Jefferson received his shipment in Washington, D.C., Lewis and his men found a well-worn Indian trail that led west up a gentle slope. A small stream ran down the hill. One of Lewis's men, Hugh McNeal, "stood with a foot on each side of this little rivulet and thanked god that he had lived to bestride the mighty & heretofore deemed endless Missouri." They were at Lemhi Pass, at the western edge of the Louisiana Territory.

Right: A black-billed magpie, unknown to science before Lewis and Clark
Far left: Lemhi Pass, on the border of Montana and Idaho

"...immence ranges of high mountains still to the West of us, with their tops partially covered with snow."

MERIWETHER LEWIS

Lewis drank from the spring and rested, then continued up the slope. He was bursting with excitement. Just a short walk ahead of him was the ridgeline, and what he believed to be the Continental Divide. On the other side, waters ran west, toward the Pacific Ocean.

If the Rocky Mountains were anything like the Appalachian Mountains back East, Lewis would top the ridge and see sprawled out before him a gentle slope, leading to a plain just like on the eastern side of the mountains. After hundreds of years of searching, the Northwest Passage would at last be found. One of the great prizes of exploration, the main reason Thomas Jefferson had sent him out West, would finally be claimed.

Lewis reached the top of the ridge, his heart pounding. He looked west, then froze. In front of Lewis were seemingly endless mountain peaks, as far as the eye could see. Lewis later wrote of the "immence ranges of high mountains still to the West of us, with their tops partially covered with snow."

The dream of the Northwest Passage, of an easy water route from coast to coast, died that day. Gone also was Lewis's hope for a quick portage to the Columbia River system. If Lewis was surprised or saddened by the harsh reality of the situation, he never recorded his feelings in his journal. Still, it must have been a shock.

But Lewis was under tremendous pressure and he didn't have time to reflect. He was separated from Clark and the rest of the expedition, with only three men at his side. A frightened horseman at that very moment was probably raising the alarm that strangers were invading Shoshone territory.

Lewis had to make contact with the Native Americans and trade for horses. The very survival of the Corps of Discovery depended on his success, and he was running out of time.

Above: A view from Lemhi Pass, looking east toward Montana *Below:* Spring wildflowers bloom on the trail leading to the Lemhi Pass

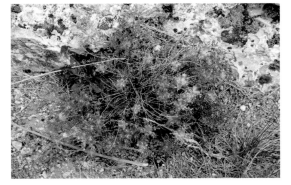

The Most Distant Fountain

"We had marched about 2 miles when we met a party of about 60 warriors mounted on excellent horses who came in nearly full speed..."

MERIWETHER LEWIS

THE SHOSHONE

After crossing the Continental Divide, Lewis and his men continued westward. They moved down the ridge, which was steeper than the east side. There were gullies and thickets, but the well-worn Indian road was easy to follow. At one point Lewis found "a handsome bold running Creek of cold water. Here I first tasted the water of the great Columbia river."

The group set up camp for a much-needed rest. But by the next day, August 13, they were up early, still following the trail down the long valley.

That morning, Lewis and his men stumbled upon three Shoshone women. One of them, a teenager, fled into the woods, but the other two, an old woman and a young girl of about 12, sat on the ground and held their heads down. They saw no chance to escape from what they thought was an Indian raiding party. Lewis wrote that they seemed ready to die.

Far Left: Newell Convers Wyeth's *Indian War Party*
Below: A photo by Andrew Russell of Shoshone warriors on horseback

Lewis took the old woman by the hand and raised her up. His arms and hands were deeply tanned from months spent in the open sunlight. So he rolled his sleeve up to show her that they were white men. He gave them some beads, mirrors, and vermilion to show the Corps was friendly. The two women were very relieved.

Suddenly, 60 Shoshone warriors came galloping up on horses. They thought they were intercepting a raiding party of Hidatsa Indians. With so many warriors, it would take only a few moments to kill Lewis and his men, if they chose to do so.

Instead of running or defending himself, Lewis ordered his men to stand still. He lowered his rifle to the ground, then followed the old Shoshone woman, who approached the lead rider. Lewis assumed this was the Shoshone chief. Lewis rolled up his sleeve to show his skin. It was the first time the Shoshone had ever seen a white man.

A deer stands in a meadow on the Lemhi Pass. Chief Cameahwait and his people eagerly accepted the gifts of meat offered by Lewis. The Shoshone at that time were on the brink of starvation.

The old woman told the chief that the strangers were friendly. She showed him the presents Lewis had given her. Tensions melted away. The chief got down off his horse and approached Lewis. He put his left arm over Lewis's right shoulder, then pressed his cheek to Lewis's and said, "Ah-hi-e." Lewis learned later the words meant "I am much pleased."

The other warriors soon joined in. Wrote Lewis, "We wer all carresed and besmeared with their grease and paint till I was heartily tired of the national hug."

The chief's name was Cameahwait, which means the One Who Never Walks. His village was very poor, having been raided earlier that spring by enemy war parties. Still, the Shoshone were generous with the newcomers. "They live in a wretched stait of poverty," wrote Lewis, but were "generous with the little they possess," and "extreemly honest."

Montana artist Charles Russell shows Lewis's first meeting with Shoshone chief Cameahwait. To show he was friendly, Lewis dropped his rifle and approached the war party, waving an American flag as a gesture of peace.

Ferns growing along the Lolo Trail in the Bitterroot Mountains

Through the sign language of George Drouillard, Lewis told Chief Cameahwait that more of his group would soon arrive, and that they needed ponies to travel over the mountains to the west. He invited Cameahwait and his warriors to go back over the Lemhi Pass and meet Clark and the rest of the Corps of Discovery. Many of Cameahwait's people thought it was a trick, that Lewis was luring their chief to an ambush. The lack of an interpreter didn't help matters. To break the language barrier, they would have to negotiate for horses with Charbonneau and Sacagawea present.

Chief Cameahwait agreed to the journey, but he grew wary of the strangers. His suspicions were eased somewhat during the hike across the Lemhi when Lewis's men killed a deer and shared it with the Shoshones. The Indians, who were half starved, gratefully accepted the meat.

On August 17, Lewis linked up with Clark and the rest of the expedition. For the men of the Corps, it was the end of dragging the canoes. They would go overland from here on, until linking up with the Columbia River system somewhere over the Bitterroot Mountains to the west.

But first, they needed ponies. The Shoshone tribe had a herd of more than 700, and Lewis was anxious to start negotiations now that he had an interpreter available. Sacagawea was called for. What happened next was one of the great coincidences of all time.

"The moccasins of the whole party were taken off, and after much ceremony the smoking began… Glad of an opportunity of being able to converse more intelligibly, Sacagawea was sent for; she came… sat down, and was beginning to interpret, when, in the person of Cameahwait, she recognized her brother. She instantly jumped up, and ran and embraced him, throwing over him her blanket, and weeping profusely."

WILLIAM CLARK

Chief Cameahwait was Sacagawea's brother. Any suspicions he had of Lewis and Clark instantly vanished. His long-lost sister had finally returned. Negotiations for the ponies began on a positive note.

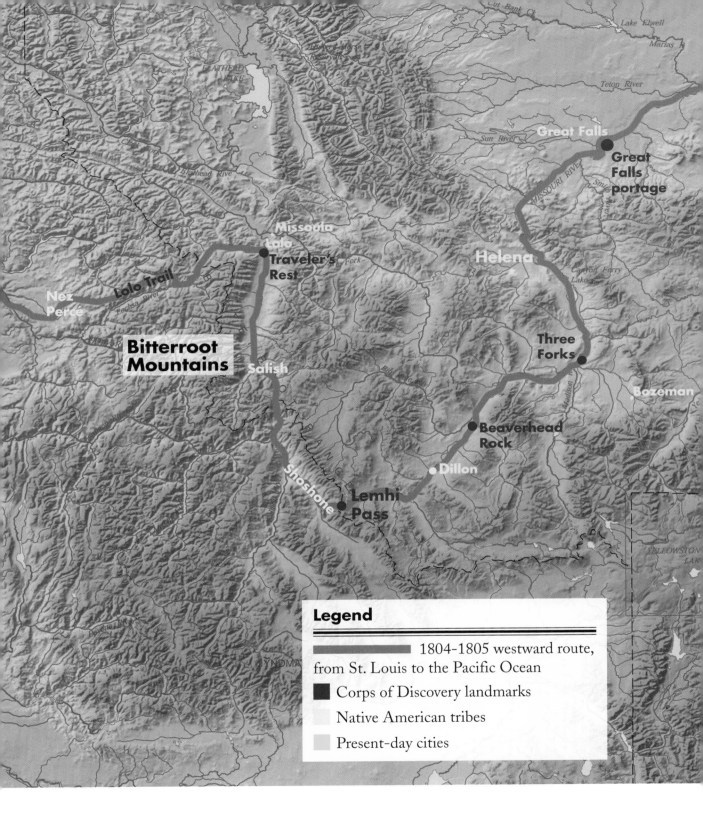

Legend

1804-1805 westward route, from St. Louis to the Pacific Ocean

Corps of Discovery landmarks

Native American tribes

Present-day cities

The Shoshone

This is a rock formation along the trail leading to the Continental Divide and Lemhi Pass. Camp Fortunate, just east of this spot, is today covered by the waters of Clark Canyon Reservoir.

Interpreting was a complicated process. The captains made an offer and passed it on to Francois Labiche, who spoke both English and French. Labiche passed the message on to Toussaint Charbonneau, who passed it on to his wife in the Hidatsa language. Sacagawea then translated the Hidatsa into Shoshone for her brother. And then the reply went back in reverse.

Despite the errors in translation that probably occurred, the captains were soon able to buy as many ponies as they needed to cross the Bitterroot Mountains. Cameahwait wanted to start good trade relations with the easterners. If, as Lewis and Clark promised, more traders followed in the years to come, Cameahwait hoped to buy much-needed guns to protect his people from the raiding parties of rival tribes.

Lewis later wrote, "Cameahwait, with his ferce eyes and lank jaws grown meager for the want of food…[said,] "If we had guns, we could live in the country of the buffaloe and eat as our enimies do, and not be compelled to hide ourselves in these mountains and live on roots and berries as the bear do."

The deal was settled. For Lewis and Clark, the waiting was over. They finally had their ponies; the trek over the mountains could begin. They were so relieved that they named their camp Camp Fortunate.

The next day, the men began the long process of portaging their supplies and equipment over the Lemhi Pass to the Shoshone village. It was August 18, Lewis's 31st birthday. He had just become the first American to cross the Continental Divide, and had finally bartered for ponies from the Shoshone so that the expedition could continue. Yet, in his journal entry that day, Lewis seemed depressed. "I had as yet done but little, very little indeed…" He vowed "in future, to live for mankind, as I have heretofore lived for myself."

Perhaps the gloomy journal entry was a sign of Lewis's depression. There had been other hints along the way, such as the long stretches of time when Lewis didn't make any journal entries at all. Lewis probably did suffer from depression, but he seldom let it affect his responsibility to the Corps. It must have taken tremendous willpower to set his feelings aside and continue leading the expedition.

Meriwether Lewis is shown in a painting by Charles Willson Peale. Even though Lewis sometimes experienced "depressions of the mind," President Jefferson had every confidence in the young Virginian. Lewis's outdoor skills and sharp powers of observation convinced the president that he was the right man to lead the Corps of Discovery.

"September 3rd Tuesday 1805
"This day we passed over emence hils
and Some of the worst roads that ever horses
passed… Our horses frequently fell… Snow
about 2 inches deep when it began to rain
which termonated in a Sleetstorm."

WILLIAM CLARK

Lewis & Clark

The Most Terrible Mountains

By early September, the Corps was on the move again. They had spent several days with the Shoshone, studying the people and their culture. But summer was quickly drawing to an end. There were mountains to be crossed.

An old Shoshone man had told Lewis about a trail that was used by the Nez Percé Indians on the western side of the mountains. The Nez Percé used the trail on their way to the Great Plains to hunt buffalo. Lewis and Clark hired the man. Old Toby, as they called him, agreed to guide the Corps to the trail and across the mountains. Sacagawea, for reasons nobody wrote down, decided to continue with the expedition instead of staying with her people.

They traveled north through rugged hills and woods. The Salmon River ran parallel to them, but they couldn't float down it. Clark had scouted ahead and reported that there were too many rapids. It was so dangerous the Indians named it the River of No Return.

Left: John Clymer's painting shows the Corps of Discovery struggling through the Bitterroot Mountains. *Right:* The River of No Return

They continued north near the border of today's Montana and Idaho. The going was rough, but they made steady progress, thanks to the 29 horses they bought from the Shoshone Indians. But whenever they looked to their left, the Bitterroot Mountains loomed over them, high and snowcapped. The men knew that soon they would turn west and cross over that seemingly impenetrable mountain barrier, or die trying.

They eventually rode over a mountain pass, then down into the valley of a beautiful river, the Bitterroot. At a place called Ross's Hole, they met a group of about 400 Salish Indians. The tribe had never seen white men before.

The Salish were friends of the Shoshone, and seeing Old Toby helped them accept the strangers. They traded with Lewis and Clark for fresh ponies. The Corps now had 39 horses, three colts, and a mule.

After following the Bitterroot River north for a few more days, the expedition stopped where Lolo Creek empties into the river. Old Toby told them that this was the spot where they would turn west and cross over the mountains. Lewis and Clark decided to camp for two days before trying to climb "those unknown formidable snow clad Mountains." They rested their horses, hunted for food, and took celestial readings for the map of the West that Clark was making for President Jefferson. Lewis called their camp Traveler's Rest.

Lewis and Clark Meeting the Flatheads at Ross' Hole, by artist Charles M. Russell. The Salish Indians were called Flatheads by Lewis and Clark. It was a name they used for many Indian tribes of the Northwest. The Salish, however, did not deform their heads like tribes along the Columbia River.

On September 11, the Corps started climbing up the Bitterroot Mountains, which Sergeant Patrick Gass called "the most terrible mountains I ever beheld."

They followed the Nez Percé path, which today is called the Lolo Trail. Even today the area is one of the most remote and wild places in the country. When the expedition went through the area, there was very little game to hunt—most animals lived down on the fertile plains. (Today, big-game animals have been driven up into the mountains by human development.) The expedition soon ran short of food. The horses were starving from a lack of grass to eat.

The trail was miserable. Fallen timber blocked the way. The ground was steep and slippery, especially when it rained. On September 14, the weather got worse and worse: rain and hail turned to sleet, then snow. Freezing wind cut through the men's clothing. Captain Clark wrote, "I have been wet and as cold in every part as I ever was in my life."

The Bitterroot Mountains almost cost the members of the Corps their lives. Lewis and Clark saw this section of the mountains to their left as they traveled north toward camp at Traveler's Rest, near present-day Missoula, Montana.

Above: Nootka Rose, growing alongside the Lolo Trail
Far right: The Lolo Trail exists today much as it did when Lewis and Clark passed through. It was an old trail used extensively by the Nez Percé, who lived west of the Bitterroot Range.

Old Toby lost the trail in the snow. Instead of following the ridgeline, he wandered down into a streambed tangled with dense brush. He eventually realized his mistake, then led the expedition back up the mountainside "as steep as the roof of a house." They lost two days because of the mistake. Still the weather worsened. Still there was nothing to eat.

To keep from starving to death they were forced to butcher one of the colts. They melted snow for drinking water. They called the stream near their camp Colt Killed Creek.

After five days of struggling over the trail, Clark climbed up a ridge and looked west. His heart sank. "From this mountain, I could observe high rugged mountains in every direction, as far as I could see."

Some of the horses, weak from exhaustion and a lack of food, slipped off the trail. Once Lewis's horse lost its footing and fell, nearly crushing the captain to death.

"September 16. When we awoke this morning, to our great surprise, we were covered with snow, which had fallen about 2 inches the later part of last night, and it continues a very cold snowstorm… Some of the men without socks, wrapped rags on their feet, and we loaded up our horses and set out without anything to eat, and proceeded on. We could hardly see the old trail for the snow."

JOSEPH WHITEHOUSE

"We came to the highest part of the mountain, we halted… The Mountains continue as far as our eyes could extend. They extend much further than we expected."

JOHN ORDWAY

This is one of many mountain streams that empty into the Lochsa River in the Bitterroot Mountains. The Lochsa runs roughly parallel to the Lolo Trail.

It was too late to turn back. In desperation, Clark and six others went ahead, trying to find food and a way out of the mountains.

The food situation grew critical. Another colt was butchered. They ate an occasional grouse, a coyote, or crayfish caught in the mountain streams. Mostly they went hungry. The men suffered from the first stages of malnutrition: weakness, skin rashes, and diarrhea. Lewis knew the expedition was on the verge of destruction. "I find myself growing weak for the want of food," he wrote, "and most of the men complain of a similar deficiency and have fallen off very much."

Frozen and nearly starved to death, the Corps of Discovery, including Sacagawea and her infant son, was forced to march onward or die in the mountains. But they were tough and disciplined, and trusted their leaders.

Finally, on September 21, they came upon a small open bottom area where there was enough grass for the horses to eat. The next day, Lewis led his men out of the mountains and into a fertile valley.

The ordeal lasted 11 torturous days, covering 160 miles (257 km) from Traveler's Rest. They wandered out of the Bitterroot wilderness half dead, more weak and vulnerable than they had ever been. But they were victorious over the mountains, thanks to their discipline, the leadership of Lewis and Clark, and the guidance of Old Toby.

But as soon as they emerged from the Bitterroots, the expedition faced another danger: the mighty Nez Percé tribe, the most powerful in the region.

As the members of the Corps staggered into a Nez Percé village, looking for food and drink, the Native Americans gathered to debate. What would they do with these strangers, these weak and hungry white men who were rich with tools and guns? Befriend them—or kill them?

Wildflowers from the Bitterroot Mountains

Famed frontier photographer Edward S. Curtis took this image of a Nez Percé warrior at the turn of the 20th century.

IF YOU GO TODAY

LEMHI PASS NATIONAL HISTORIC LANDMARK

Lemhi Pass straddles the Continental Divide on the Montana-Idaho border. It is the site where Meriwether Lewis discovered there was no easy water route from coast to coast. Instead, when he reached the top of the ridgeline, he later wrote, "I discovered immence ranges of high mountains still to the West of us with their tops partially covered with snow." Lemhi Pass today is much as it was when the Corps of Discovery passed by in 1805. It is about 22 miles (35 km) west of the town of Grant, Montana, on a dusty, bumpy road that can be difficult to drive on, especially after a rainstorm. The U.S. Forest Service maintains signposts showing Lewis's route.

BEAVERHEAD ROCK STATE PARK, MT

Beaverhead Rock is a landmark that Sacagawea recognized as the Corps struggled up the Jefferson River. It is still visible today. Beaverhead Rock State Park is located just a few miles north of the town of Dillon, Montana.

LOLO TRAIL

Along with Lemhi Pass and a small section of the Missouri River east of Fort Benton, Montana, the Lolo Trail is very close to how Lewis and Clark saw it in 1805. Access is off U.S. Highway 12 west of Lolo, Montana. A small section of the actual trail can be hiked near Highway 12, but most of the Lolo follows a ridgeline north of the road. Also on Highway 12 is the Lolo Visitor Center, which has interpretive exhibits. The trail is open only during the summer months, July through September.

GLOSSARY

CORPS

A branch of the military that has a specialized function.

GREAT PLAINS

A huge, sloping region of valleys and plains in west-central North America. The Great Plains extend from Texas to southern Canada, and from the Rocky Mountains nearly 400 miles (644 km) to the east.

PASS

A path used to cross a mountain ridge that divides two watersheds. For example, the Lemhi Pass crosses the Continental Divide—water running down the east side finds its way to the Atlantic Ocean, while water on the west side flows to the Pacific Ocean. Passes are usually low points between two higher peaks. "Divide" and "saddle" are other words for pass.

PIROGUE

A large, canoe-shaped boat, used to carry cargo, that is powered by oars, or sometimes a sail. The Corps of Discovery used two pirogues.

PORTAGE

To carry a boat and supplies overland from one lake or river to another. The Corps of Discovery portaged around the Great Falls of Montana for over 18 miles (29 km).

WEB SITES

Would you like to learn more about Lewis & Clark? Please visit **www.abdopub.com** to find up-to-date Web site links about Lewis & Clark and the Corps of Discovery. These links are routinely monitored and updated to provide the most current information available.

INDEX